God's Sustaining Hand

~ A life of Hope ~

Diane Rodriguez-Burton

God's Sustaining Hand

~ A life of Hope ~

Copyright © 2023 **Diane Rodriguez-Burton**

All rights reserved. No part of this publication may be reproduced, distributed, or transmitted in any form or by any means, including photocopying, recording, or other electronic or mechanical methods, without the prior written permission of the publisher, except in the case of brief quotations embodied in critical reviews and certain other noncommercial uses permitted by copyright law. For permission requests, write to the publisher, addressed "Attention: Book Rights and Permission," at the address below.

Published in the United States of America

ISBN 978-1-961507-82-1 (SC)
ISBN 978-1-962110-31-0 (HC)
ISBN 978-1-962110-32-7 (Ebook)

Diane Rodriguez-Burton
222 West 6th Street
Suite 400, San Pedro, CA, 90731
drodriguezburton@yahoo.com

Order Information and Rights Permission:

Quantity sales. Special discounts might be available on quantity purchases by corporations, associations, and others. For details, contact the publisher at the address above.

For Book Rights Adaptation and other Rights Permission. Call us at toll-free 1-888-945-8513 or send us an email at admin@stellarliterary.com.

Table of Contents

Dedication vii

Introduction ix

Forward xi

Preface xiii

I Am A Child But No One Seems To Care 1

Bullies Are Mean People 3

God Kept me 5

Abandonment Steals But God Provides 7

Love Should Not Hurt 9

Watch out for Wolves in Sheep Clothing 11

A life of Hope 13

The Lord Strengthens 15

Abundant Living is from the Lord 17

My life is in God's Hand 19

Author's Note 23

Dedication

This book is dedicated back to God for keeping and bringing me through trying situations, perilous times and to this moment of peace that surpasses all understanding.

To all the people who have lived through difficult times by holding on to their faith in God and hope for a glorious eternal life and well-being; and lastly, to those who may also be going through trials and tribulations yet holding on and rekindling the fire of their faith as they are reminded that God's hand is a mighty sustaining anchor through illnesses. As she understood how the Lord had always rescued her from the enemy's schemes and saved her life, she continually exercised her offering of gratitude to God through praise and worship through a one-on-one sustaining relationship.

Introduction

When asked about my childhood and young adult experience, I say, "It was rough, but I lived to grow beyond it. I know not my mother as a mother, even when she was living with me she never showed me love!" I didn't know much about God because my parents didn't go to church. We never went to church like other families, in fact the only time I ever went to church was during the summers I was allowed to visit Grandma in North Carolina. I remember asking God, why is my life so painful and demoralizing?" I came to know God's sustaining hand in my life. I had hope and the Lord faithfully kept me.

Forward

Mrs. Henrietta Patrice Evans is a member of our Congregation, where she serves in her Calling as a Mother at the Greater Works Baptist Church, Inc. of Jonesboro, Georgia. My purpose for penning this autobiographical account of her life is to honor her request to write and publish her testimony as an encouragement to anyone who may be going through tough times and feel that they are dying inside. She wants you, the readers, to know that God is more than just the creator of all things, including life; but, with Him, you can and will survive victoriously. Since the Lord is all knowing, ever-present, as well as all intelligence, He is the sustainer of life. No matter what you may be going through, He is able to keep you, just like He has kept her. Another reason for her life's story is to let everyone know that forgiveness is necessary. The word of God teaches that every person needs forgiveness, and every person needs to forgive. We need God's grace and must be willing to extend that same mercy to others no matter what they may have done to us.

I have forgiven everyone who has ever hurt me because of **Matthew 6:14-15** which states:

"For if ye forgive men their trespasses, your heavenly Father will also forgive you: But if ye forgive not men their trespasses, neither will your Father forgive your trespasses."

We have all sinned, fallen short of God's glory, and need God's forgiveness!

~ Rev. Diane Rodriguez – Burton

Preface

"And I give unto them eternal life; and they shall never perish, neither shall any man pluck them out of my hand."
(John 10:28)

This book is an Autobiography of Henrietta Patrice Evans. Mother Henrietta Patrice Evans was born a bi-racial child in a small rural town in the Deep South. Having been brought into the world in a low-income family setting by parents who believed that moving north to the city of brotherly love meant a better life, their plight worsened, and for her, life got worst! By the grace of God, she was able to overcome tremendous hardship experiences.

Her life's story testifies to how the Lord kept and provided for her throughout the mid-20th century well into the 21st century. A life that began lowly and became increasingly better during the latter years, even as she suffered through her many illnesses.

As she thought about her life and the difficulties of being abused and misused by those who were supposed to love her, she began to understand how the Lord had always rescued her from the enemy's schemes. It was God who had saved her life repeatedly; this is why she continually exercised her offering of gratitude to God through praise and worship. In hearing and obeying that still small voice to look up to Him, God has kept her through a one-on-one sustaining relationship.

I am a Child But No One Seems to Care

Reflecting on my life, I can see God's Sustaining Hand in every area. I didn't always know the Lord through the pardoning of my sins, but I can't help but thank Him for knowing all about me, loving me when I did not love myself, and keeping me. I had a very tough childhood and young adult life, but I now recognize that the Lord saved and kept me alive! I was born Henrietta Patrice Moses to Mr. Edward Arden Moses and Mrs. Harriett Pauline on a chilly February 13th morning in 1950 in Hertford County in Hertford, North Carolina. Hertford is a small town. My father was a poor White man and my mother was Black and poor. When I was a child, Hertford was somewhat quiet, undiscovered, and overlooked by casual visitors speeding along to the more populated inner banks towns of Elizabeth City or Edenton, also located in the northeastern corner of the state. During my childhood, Black folks were limited in where they could go, the facilities they could frequent, and the time they could be outdoors. We had to walk on one side of the street. It did not matter that I am bi-racial. That made life worst.

~ *Diane Rodriguez Butron* ~

I remember the Woolworth Department store's soda fountain counter so well and the restrictions against people of color. We were not allowed to sit at the counter because we were not White. This was also during the time when water fountains and restrooms were clearly marked as "White only" or "Others!"

My dad left us when I was only twelve years old, and when I turned thirteen, we eventually had to move from our house into lower-rent project housing. As the oldest child to three younger siblings at the time, I was automatically appointed the house's resident babysitter and caretaker. Times were hard, and as my dad sought better employment wages, we moved from Hertford, North Carolina, to Philadelphia, Pennsylvania, right after I was 9 years old. I was able to pick up babysitting jobs and earned an average of $15.00 a week, most of which my mother took.

Although I worked as a babysitter, I was also responsible for grocery shopping, cooking and feeding the family, and performing all house chores. My mother viewed me as the family's built-in servant, not as a child.

Within two and a half years, Momma had two outside pregnancies.

Now I was the eldest of four sisters and one brother. I yearned to visit Grandma in North Carolina, but unfortunately, such visits became fewer and fewer until one-day Grandma went to Heaven to be with the Lord, which I had learned about at her church. I was the eldest of four sisters and one brother. I yearned to visit Grandma in North Carolina, but unfortunately, such visits became fewer and fewer until one-day Grandma went to Heaven to be with the Lord, whom I had learned about at her church.

I missed her since she seemed to have been the only person who remembered and thought of me as a child.

Bullies Are Mean People

Times were hard for me. Whenever Momma went downtown shopping, she always returned with clothing for herself and my younger siblings. I can't ever remember receiving anything new from her. I only had two dresses that had been given to me by my grandmother, and even then, my mother would wear them. I, unfortunately, had to alternate between those two dresses to dress for school. When they were new, she wore them first. I had to wash out stains of whichever one Momma wasn't wearing.

I hated going to school because the other children teased and made fun of my clothing and shoes. My shoes had holes in the soles, and I had to cut cardboard and place it inside to keep my old socks or feet from rubbing the ground. I never felt pretty growing up, and reflecting on those early days, I never really had a childhood. Growing up, and reflecting on those early days, I never really had a childhood.

I had to comb my hair and everybody else's in the house; this meant going to sleep later than everyone as well as getting up before anyone else to prepare for the day. I stayed inside as much as possible because I didn't have pretty clothes or shoes to wear to public venues. I did not have friends in my age group, so naturally, I had low self-esteem. Momma made me go to the store, and I had to walk my younger siblings wherever they needed to go. I had to rush home to wash, cook and clean up the house, then watch out for my sisters and brother ensuring their safe return home and comfort.

When I was 14 years old, I found it disgusting being forced to collect old beer bottles from our house and go out savaging to find other empty beer bottles to carry to the local package and liquor store for nickels to buy alcohol. I constantly had to buy more beer and bring it home for Momma. No one ever questioned my age when I bought alcohol. No one even considered that I may not have been old enough to even purchase alcohol. I wondered whether laws were too lax, merchants didn't care because they just wanted to make a sale, or they assumed I was an adult because of my size and mature-looking figure. Maybe I was the scapegoat for performing the petty things my parent wanted to appease her miserable lifestyle.

God Kept me

My mother entertained boyfriends and often purchased new fancy outfits to wear when she went out to party at the Cabaret on the weekends with my earnings from babysitting. When she was intoxicated and not paying attention, her boyfriends' often tried to touch my body and push up against and handle me, so I had to fight to get out of their grasp to escape their rape attempts. I also had to protect my sister, who was close to my age. When I would tell Momma, she would get so angry with me! She said I was lying and accused me of enticing her boyfriends.

I may not have been in church, but I would pray, Lord, save me, and He did because I managed to get away from those men. I started hiding whenever Momma had a man in the house. I'd hide in closets, behind our bed, and sometimes in the bathroom with the door locked for protection.

The world becomes jaded when you are in some family structure with people you're supposed to trust to help and protect you, who are live-in adversaries. When perpetrators threaten and violate you, they side with the perpetrators. I was determined to defend myself and my siblings. Momma seemed to have blinders regarding my younger sibling's well-being, which made me automatically responsible for their safety.

I recall one day when I was about twelve and a half years old, I cleaned the house, cooked the meal, and fed the other children, and I even prepared a nice plate for Momma and stored it in a special cupboard to retain the freshness.

I washed everyone's clothes on the washboard and hung them on clotheslines outside to dry, hoping to please my mother. She was ungrateful and punished me for moving things around in the living room. Grandma taught me always to respect my elders, and I did, even though; I felt unloved, unappreciated, and abandoned in our house. I prayed to God every day for protection and strength. I learned later that it was Him who kept me.

Abandonment Steals But God Provides

My mother left us and moved to New York, following behind a man. Believe it or not, Momma became a purposeful absentee parent. All the children were left home for me to raise in the projects with no provisions. I was almost fifteen years old, so legally I wasn't a foundling, but my siblings were because they were 12, nearly 13 years old, and under.

We lived in poverty, so life was hard, even though I had always managed to care for the younger kids. I guess no one reported us to the authorities because no one came to visit from an orphanage. Although we were physically abandoned, I suffered more from the emotional abandonment I had felt when I was a young child.

Emotional and psychological wounds are deep-rooted. I am sure my younger siblings were also hurting deeply and probably feel that pain today which is why we have trust issues and never had a close relationship as sibling friends into adulthood. God's hands sustain each of us and it is my prayer that healing will come and true bonding will take place before any of us pass on to glory. I know that all things are possible and this to will come to fruition if we can come together and focus in faith.

During the time Momma physically abandoned us, I was grateful that we still had a place to sleep, and government food subsidies that applied.

That government cheese was the best block of cheese I have ever tasted, and I could make that spam taste just like a delicious plump ham. Abandonment does steal; however, I realize that God was and still is the source of my provisions.

Love Should Not Hurt

I met and had my first boyfriend at age fifteen, his name was Thomas McKay. I was starving for love and affection since my mother withheld those vital emotional and spiritual needs from me. When Thomas showed me a little attention I thought that I was in love! Phew, finally someone paid attention to me. He was charming and complimentary, he said he admired how well I took care of my siblings and myself and my mother's apartment. He even said I looked good to him. We became physically intimate and during my emotional and new found experience, I conceived. I contacted Momma and told her I was pregnant and she was very angry. My baby was born when I was sixteen and Momma made me marry Thomas. During that time "Shotgun" weddings were common place when an unwedded girl got pregnant.

Momma had to take my youngest siblings with her after the baby arrived. Thereafter I had two more babies; our children were stair steps one after another. My husbands aggressive and cruel nature became an almost daily occurrence as he brutally beat and cursed me.

He may have broken down my body with constant physical battering, but he could not destroy my spirit. Later as I pondered this thought, I knew that the Lord had me in His sustaining hand. In order to protect myself, once again I found myself hiding in the house, locked in the bathroom and sleeping in the bathtub with the babies. The times would come when my husband would not only beat me, but would draw a gun and shoot at me throughout the house. It was by the grace of God that he was not able to kill me and the babies.

I Corinthians 13 says; Love is kind

I knew that Love should not and would not hurt. I soon realized that what my husband and I had was not love. Thank God my siblings were older and had gone on to New York with my mother because things turned ugly and got to be extremely dangerous over the years.

We had never had a formal family reunion, but one day, I seized the opportunity as I had $5.00 in my hand; I quickly dressed, got a ride to the bus depot, and took the babies to New York, where Momma was. Momma offered no refuge; she said I was not welcome there and made me return home to my husband. After being married to him for ten years, he was killed in a car accident. It again dawned on me that nobody but the Lord had kept me, rescued me, and, most of all, saved me because Jesus truly does love me. I wasn't in a church, but I began to reflect on the Lord's title of Jehovah Jireh, which means; He was and is my provider! The housing project and meals, including government cheese, spam, etc., were one of the means that the Lord had provided for me and my family, which sustained us during a trying and challenging time(s) of my life.

Watch out for Wolves in Sheep's Clothing

After my husband's death, Thomas McKay, I finally moved to New York; after all, I had no known family left in Philadelphia. I initially moved in with Momma, but that was very short-lived, as I received Social Security and moved to Brooklyn, New York. I applied and was blessed to get a job at a Brooklyn department store, which paid a decent salary. For the first time in my life, I could afford nice-looking clothes for my children and me, and we dressed well. I started going to church, joined and got my children baptized and regularly attended worship service, and began working with ministries within the church. I confided in the church officials to include the Deacons and Deaconess Board. The Pastor had recently lost his wife, of whom I had never met. Since I was new and widowed, he invited me and my children to dinner.

The following Sunday, he announced to the congregation that God had given him a new wife, and then he had me stand and presented me as his new wife.

He thought I had money. He had had someone he knew prepare and sign a phony marriage license. His proposal or marriage ceremony was nothing we had discussed or planned, although I was too shy, timid, respectful, and shocked to say anything before his congregation. I thought the man had really received a message from God, and of course, I truly craved true love, even though it did not feel quite right to me. We went to a Clergyman's Convention the next week, which was out of the area, and while we were gone, his house caught on fire and burned down. His adult niece lived in the basement of his house and could get my children out to safety. He thought I had enough money to repair his home or help him with a new place to live. I did not have that kind of money and told him I could not help him. He was visibly angry, and it was apparent that he had no real love for me. All I ever wanted was for someone to love me. I quickly got away from him and out of his church and thanked God for protecting me and allowing me to see that this man was not of Him;

Instead of being Christ-like, he acted more like the devil. He was a wolf in sheep's clothing!

I found a new job but did not keep it very long because I couldn't shake the feeling and fear that someone was always following me.

I was so paranoid, almost to the point of feeling paralyzed, because I didn't want any physical harm to come to me or my children. I lost my job as I could not get there without looking over my shoulder and hiding out. The Lord had to strengthen me through reading His Word and daily Prayer.

A Life of Hope

In 1974, I was introduced to my current husband, a native of West Africa, by a friend who lived in my apartment complex in Brooklyn, New York; he was also a relative of my friend's husband. I discovered he was seeking a short-term marriage arrangement to apply for American citizenship and avoid deportation back to West Africa, as his Visa had expired. He was employed with the prestigious North Shore Tower and wanted to keep his good-paying job. English was not his native language, so he spoke broken English but understood it much better. When he said to me;

"I want to hire you to marry me for a brief time until I receive U.S citizenship."

If I decide to marry you, it must be legally and spiritually binding, following God's law!"

We dated for five months, and after being engaged for three weeks, we married and moved to Queens, New York.

Since my husband was from a different culture, we had much to learn about each other during the early years. I helped him with the appropriate immigration paperwork; so he could submit it with our legally binding document. I am so grateful that God has blessed our marriage union for 43 years and counting.

The Lord Strengthens

Although no children resulted from our consummation, we understood that we were tremendously blessed since I had four healthy children from my previous marriage, and he had three. My children were already with us, but his children were in West Africa. It took five years to get his children to the States, but they made it, and with seven children, we were like the Brady bunch. I raised seven children, yet no one calls me Mommy. In the beginning, my children did not care for their new Dad; well, of course, they wouldn't; because they did not want anyone new coming into our lives. As time passed, we bonded as a family to establish healthy relations as our children grew up.

Abundant Living is from the Lord

After living in Queens, New York, for 32 years in our first house/home together, my husband and I packed up our household and moved to Baltimore, Maryland. I chose Baltimore, hoping to interact with relatives who had made it their home years earlier. I found a church home and joined. After a couple of years in Baltimore, one of my husband's family members who lived in Georgia passed away. We went to Georgia to attend the funeral that summer, and even though we came for a solemn occasion, we liked it. The following summer, we returned to Georgia to visit my stepdaughter and enjoyed the Atlanta suburb where she resides. While there, we met a lady whose husband worked for a local realtor company. He had heard we pondered the idea of making Georgia our new home. The inquiring lady arranged for him to show us a couple of houses. I fell in love with the second house on Jonesboro Road; we purchased it, and this is still our home today.

Shortly after moving in, I searched for a new church home and found myself in a number of large and even diverse congregations. The physical buildings were beautiful and prestigious looking, but I wasn't comfortable at any of them. I kept praying to God to lead me to the fellowship where I could freely Worship Him. After a couple of months of visiting church after church and a couple of them twice, I saw this little stony old fashion looking church building on a hill on Walt Stephens Road ten minutes from our house. I slowed down and read the sign, Greater Works Baptist Church. Under the name of the church I read, "Come and grow with us." I decided to turn in to the drive way for a visit. As I entered the doors, I encountered the warmth of smiling faces and greetings with loving embraces. I sat and became a participant in the Sunday school class; I freely praised God during the 11:00 a.m. Worship Service and was made to feel comfortable by the sister who gave the Welcome. I felt compelled to introduce myself as I soaked up the loving fellowship and encouraging Word of God. I knew for certain that this little church fellowship was where I was meant to be.

My life is in God's Hand

Mother Evans brought a wholesome spirit to our church. We have a small but growing congregation at Greater Works of Jonesboro, GA. She joined and said, "My Calling after Salvation is that of Ushering. My life is in God's hand". Immediately, thought about scripture that I often meditate on in the book of Psalm. **Psalm 84:9-11** (*How lovely are Your Dwellings!*) It states:

> *"9 Behold our shield, O God, And look*
> *upon the face of Your anointed.*
> *10 For a day in Your courts is better than*
> *a thousand outside. I would rather stand at the*
> *threshold of the house of my God*
> *than dwell in the tents of wickedness.*
> *11 For the LORD God is a sun and shield;*
> *The LORD gives grace and glory;*
> *No good thing does He withhold*
> *from those who walk uprightly."*

She served well as a warm and elegant Usher for nine years, and after observing her walk with Christ and her remarkable character, we knew that the Lord wanted to elevate her for greater service.

The church formerly appointed her and two other godly female members to serve as our church Mothers; their appointments formalized the GWBC Mother's Board.

The Apostle Paul, in both (***I Corinthians 12***) and (***Romans 12***), informs us that the church being members of one body, exemplifies the body of Christ, of which Christ Himself is the head. Each member is an integral part of the body that must depend on each other part/member to function correctly. Mother Evans was and is a God-sent member who fits right in with our local body at Greater Works **(*GWBC*)**. In 2011 she was awarded and presented GWBC's second quarterly Certificate of Appreciation, which reads:

> *"This Certificate is presented to Sister Henrietta P. Evans,*
> *for her thoughtfulness and unselfish service and support*
> *to Greater Works' Baptist Church vision."*

She has served as head Usher/Door Keeper for the last seven years and in the spirit of meeting and greeting and assisting in this role she used her creative gift and skills for esthetic beauty to create the decorative baskets seen around the Church and in our Fellowship Hall. She designed and donated the lovely vase bouquets in the windows of the church and created the beautiful Christmas wreaths that were enjoyed by all who visited during the Christmas holiday season.

She volunteered her time and gifts in support of a variety of Church activities in a most unselfish manner. Sister Evan's thoughtful assistance not only exemplifies the Greater Works Baptist Church's motto of:

"***We Are the Hands of God***", best exemplifies her willingness and efforts to perform greater works as relayed in (***John 14:12***). We would like to personally thank her for assisting us along with other generous members of our congregation and enabling us to make great strides in making both members and visitors feel welcome and comfortable in this our church!

We are honored to present this certificate of appreciation as a means of saying that she makes a difference in the body of Christ. We thank her and pray God's continual blessings over her efforts and willingness to serve within His Divine favor.

In Christ's Love,

 ***CHURCH VISION:***

"Like Minded" … "Same Passion"…
"One God"
(Mat 28:19-20; Acts 1-8)

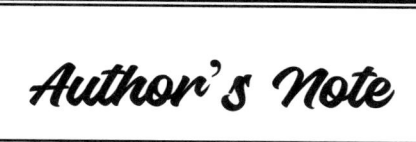

Author's Note

Thank you, Mother Henrietta Evans, for entrusting me with such a delicate and personal aspect of your life. You could have enlisted the services of numerous other writers, yet you chose and asked me to write and publish your Autobiography in book form. Hopefully, the Lord utilized my skills to prepare a dignified and professional document that will encourage others, glorify God, and serve as a product you will be proud of. I admire your courage to use your personal life experiences to reach the masses, informing some and reminding others that we are all important to God.

Your life demonstrates how the Lord will never leave nor forsake us. Many who may feel hopeless will become hopeful just by knowing and acting upon the call to accept the way of Christianity. Accept and believe that God loves them and that His word informs all that the Lord Jesus laid down His life so they might live. My Faith is continually increasing through testimonies such as yours! I know that I matter because God loves me, and I am not alone; I know that I can call on the name of Jesus anytime and anywhere. His hands sustain me! Again, thank you!

Reverend Diane Rodriguez-Burton
Assistant Pastor
Greater Works Baptist Church, Inc.
Jonesboro, Georgia

Printed by Libri Plureos GmbH in Hamburg, Germany